The United States

Arkansas

Anne Welsbacher
ABDO & Daughters

visit us at
www.abdopub.com

Published by Abdo & Daughters, 4940 Viking Drive, Suite 622, Edina, Minnesota 55435.
Copyright © 1998 by Abdo Consulting Group, Inc., Pentagon Tower, P.O. Box 36036,
Minneapolis, Minnesota 55435 USA. International copyrights reserved in all countries.
No part of this book may be reproduced in any form without written permission from the
publisher.

Printed in the United States.

Cover and Interior Photo credits: SuperStock, Archive Photos

Edited by Lori Kinstad Pupeza
Contributing editor Brooke Henderson
Special thanks to our Checkerboard Kids—Annie O'Leary, Morgan Roberts, Teddy
Borth, Tyler Wagner

All statistics taken from the 1990 census; The Rand McNally Discovery Atlas of The
United States. Other Sources: Arkansas, Children's Press, Chicago, 1994; Arkansas,
Children's Press, Chicago, 1989; Arkansas, Lerner Publications Co., Minneapolis, 1994;
America Online, Compton's Encyclopedia, 1990; World Book Encyclopedia.

Library of Congress Cataloging-in-Publication Data

Welsbacher, Anne, 1955-
      Arkansas / Anne Welsbacher.
      p.   cm. -- (United States)
      Includes Index.
      Summary: Surveys the people, geography, and history of southern state known
      as the Land of Opportunity.
      ISBN 1-56239-852-0
      1. Arkansas--Juvenile literature. [1. Arkansas.] I. Title. II. Series: United States
      (Series)
      F411.3.W45 1998
      976.7--dc21   97-10048
                                                                     CIP
                                                                     AC

Contents

Welcome to Arkansas

Arkansas is one of the southern states of the United States. It is called the Land of Opportunity.

Arkansas has mountains, valleys, and lakes. It is famous for its hot springs. It has the only diamond mine in the United States! Many people visit the springs, lakes, and mines of Arkansas.

Arkansans elected the first woman to become a United States senator. President Clinton is from Arkansas. And writer Maya Angelou grew up in Arkansas.

Opposite page: Bath House Row in Hot Springs, Arkansas, where tourists come for the mineral waters.

Fast Facts

ARKANSAS

Capital and largest city
Little Rock (175,795 people)
Area
52,082 square miles
(134,892 sq km)
Population
2,362,239 people
Rank: 33rd
Statehood
June 15, 1836
(25th state admitted)
Principal rivers
Arkansas River,
Mississippi River,
White River
Highest point
Magazine Mountain;
2,753 feet (839 m)
Motto
Regnat populus
(The people rule)
Song
"Arkansas"
Famous People
President Bill Clinton, Hattie
Caraway, Johnny Cash, James W.
Fulbright, Douglas MacArthur

State Flag

Apple Blossom

Mockingbird

Pine

About Arkansas

The Natural State

Detail area

Arkansas' abbreviation

Borders: west (Oklahoma, Texas), north (Missouri),
east (Tennessee, Mississippi), south (Louisiana)

Nature's Treasures

Arkansas has many **minerals** in both the land and water! Arkansas is famous for its hot springs. The hot springs are like giant bathtubs filled with warm water. Many people come to Arkansas just to soak in its hot springs.

Some of the springs also have minerals in the water. These minerals make the water feel good.

Arkansas also has rich soil. There is good farmland along the rivers and in the valleys. About half the state has farms on it. Arkansas is warm and moist in the summer, and cool in the winter.

Arkansas has many rivers. The Mississippi River flows along its east border. The Arkansas River cuts across the center and then turns south. It meets the Mississippi River near the bottom of the state.

There are many lakes in Arkansas. Some were formed by dams built by people. Others were formed naturally. Lake Chicot was formed by a river! It changed its course and this created a lake. This kind of lake is called an **oxbow lake**.

The Arkansas River at sun down.

Beginnings

Arkansas was once under water! Fish **fossils** have been found in Arkansas. Early Arkansans were **Native Americans** who lived in caves and **bluffs**. They lived 12,000 years ago! One of the groups was called the Quapaw. They were called the Arkansas by the French.

Explorers came in the 1500s and 1600s. In 1803, the French sold Arkansas and other areas to the United States. In the 1800s, settlers arrived from nearby states. They forced the Native Americans to move west.

In 1836, Arkansas became a state. Settlers, along with their slaves, were moving to Arkansas. By the 1860s, one out of every four people in Arkansas were slaves.

In the 1860s, many southern states **seceded** from the United States. Southern states wanted slavery. Northern states did not. This led to the Civil War.

Arkansas was **divided** over slavery. At first Arkansas decided to stay with the United States. But in 1861 it decided to **secede**.

The northern states won the Civil War. In the 1870s, the North tried to help the South rebuild. This was called **Reconstruction**. In 1877 the North stopped helping the South.

African Americans were no longer slaves. But they still did not have the same rights as white people. In the 1940s, 1950s, and 1960s, the Civil Rights movement was born. People fought for equal rights for African Americans. These rights included **integration** and voting rights.

A Civil War battle scene.

B.C. to 1600

Native Americans: The First Arkansans

 10,000 B.C.: Bluff-dwelling Native Americans live in cliffs and bluffs of Arkansas.

 25 B.C.: Mound-building Native Americans live in Arkansas area. They build huge mounds.

 1600s: Osage, Caddos, and Quapaw peoples live in Arkansas. French explorers came in the late 1600s.

Arkansas

B.C. to 1600

1800s

A Stormy Century

 1803: France sells its land in Arkansas to the United States.

 1800s: Settlers from nearby states force **Native Americans** west. Settlers bring slaves.

 1836: Arkansas becomes a state.

 1861: Arkansas votes to remain with the United States. Then it votes to **secede** from the United States. The Civil War begins.

 1865-1877: The **reconstruction** period.

14

Arkansas
1800s

1900s

Times of Change

1921: Oil is discovered in Arkansas.

1940s-1960s: The Civil Rights movement works for equal rights.

1957: U.S. Supreme Court forces all-white school in Little Rock to allow African-American students to enter. Troops have to be used to enforce the law.

1970: Arkansas River program opens river to boaters from Mississippi River to Oklahoma.

Arkansas
1900s

Arkansas's People

There are more than two million people in Arkansas. Half live in cities, half live on farms or in small towns. Many people living in Arkansas moved there to **retire**.

One out of every six Arkansans are African American. Most are white. A few Arkansans are **Latinos**, **Native Americans**, and Asian Americans.

Arkansans are very different from each other. Arkansans in the south of the state call themselves southerners. Arkansans in the west part of the state call themselves westerners. People who live in the mountains think of themselves much like their neighbors in Missouri.

President Bill Clinton is from Arkansas. He was born in Hope, Arkansas. Johnny Cash is from Arkansas.

His family grew cotton when he was a boy. He wrote his first song when he was 12!

Baseball player Brooks Robinson is from Arkansas. He is in the Baseball Hall of Fame. Singer Glen Campbell also is from Arkansas.

Brooks Robinson

President Bill Clinton

Johnny Cash

Splendid Cities

The largest city in Arkansas is Little Rock. Little Rock also is the capital of Arkansas. It has many parks and old buildings. It is near the middle of the state.

President Clinton was born in Hope, Arkansas. Hope is near a diamond mine. It also is called the Watermelon Capital. It has a Watermelon Festival every year.

Texarkana is between Arkansas and Texas. It actually is two cities. One is in Arkansas. The other is in Texas. The post office is on State Line Avenue. It is right in the middle!

Little Rock

Hope

Texarkana

Little Rock, Arkansas.

Arkansas's Land

Arkansas is shaped like a cup. That is a good shape for it, because it has lots of water! It is the smallest state west of the Mississippi River.

Arkansas has many mountains. The Ozark Mountains are very beautiful. Other mountains in Arkansas are Ouachita Mountains and the Boston Mountains.

Forests fill about half of the state. Ash, basswood, elm, hickory, oak, wild cherry, and willow are some of the trees in Arkansas. Flowers like orchids and yellow jasmines grow wild in Arkansas. There also are ferns. One kind of fern that grows in Arkansas is very **rare**.

Bobcats, deer, foxes, and rabbits run through the fields and forests of Arkansas. Muskrats, raccoons, and skunks live in the mountains.

Arkansas also has quail, wild ducks, wild geese, and wild turkeys. It has songbirds like blue jays and cardinals. And it has reptiles like lizards, turtles, and snakes.

A lot of Arkansas is filled with forests and mountains.

Arkansas at Play

Arkansas is like a big playground. That's because Arkansas has many rivers, lakes, forests, and parks. Many people fish in Arkansas. They catch lots of trout.

People also boat, ski, canoe, and swim in Arkansas's waters. They also can hike in the forests and parks. At one park, you can mine for diamonds, and keep any diamonds you find!

Many Arkansas parks and museums tell about its history. One museum shows guns used by Jesse James, Pancho Villa, and Annie Oakley. Many people like folk music in Arkansas, too. You can hear folk and country music at the Original Ozark Folk Festival in Eureka Springs.

Arkansans are "hog-wild" for football! The University of Arkansas football team is called the **Razorbacks**. A razorback is a kind of **hog**. Razorback fans call out "wooooo pig SOO-eee!" when they go to games!

There are many **annual** events in Arkansas. You can visit the rodeo, a duck calling festival, or a horse race. There also are flower festivals and peach festivals.

The rodeo is popular in Arkansas.

Arkansas at Work

Many Arkansans work in **manufacturing**. Arkansans make and package many foods, like chicken and rice. They also make paper, wood products, and clothing.

Another form of work in Arkansas is farming. More chickens are raised in Arkansas than in any other state! Arkansas also sells many eggs. Can you guess why?

Many people work in mining. They mine for gas and oil. They also mine **bromine**.

Opposite page:
Chicken farming is big
business in Arkansas.

Fun Facts

•The post office in Texarkana lists both Texas and Arkansas in its mailing address.

•The "hanging judge" Isaac Parker sentenced 160 men to death (79 were actually killed) in Arkansas during the wild west days in the 1800s.

•In the 1800s, people argued over how to say the name Arkansas. Some called it Ar-KAN-sus. Others called it AR-kan-saw. In 1881 a law was passed. The state is said as AR-kan-saw. But it is spelled Arkansas!

•There is a town called Yellville, named after an Arkansas governor named Archibald Yell. Yellville hosts an annual turkey calling contest.

•The name Arkansas comes from a Native American word. It means "land of down-stream people."

Opposite page: Arkansas has cowboys.

Glossary

Annual: happening once every year.

Bluff: a cliff, a steep, rocky area.

Bromine: a mineral used to make dye and medicine.

Divided: to have different beliefs about something.

Fossil: a very old body of a once-living animal, fish, or plant. The body has turned into a hard substance like a rock.

Hog: a kind of pig.

Integration: to include people of all races.

Latino: people who came to the United States from Central America and South America.

Minerals: things in the earth like coal or gold that have to be mined or dug out of the ground.

Manufacture: to make things.

Native Americans: the first people to occupy America.

Oxbow Lake: a kind of lake caused by a river bending back in a new direction.

Rare: very few in the world.

Razorback: a kind of hog.

Reconstruction: a time in U.S. history following the Civil War. The North helped the South rebuild their houses, land, and jobs.

Retire: to stop working.

Secede: to break away.

Internet Sites

Arkansas Showcase
http://www.cris.com/~Talewins
Arkansas Showcase is an organized hubsite designed with the new surfer in mind. Each spoke from this page leads to a hub of other pages with personally evaluated links and features found nowhere else. From our hubs here you will find spokes leading to every major Show Stopping Site in Arkansas.

Famous Arkansans
http://www.ualr.edu/~blwestbrook/arkansas
I'm sure most people (at least in America) are aware that President Clinton hails from Arkansas. What you may not know, however, is that there are and have been many famous people who at one time or another called Arkansas home. This site lists a few of them.

These sites are subject to change. Go to your favorite search engine and type in Arkansas for more sites.

PASS IT ON

Tell Others Something Special About Your State

To educate readers around the country, pass on interesting tips, places to see, history, and little unknown facts about the state you live in. We want to hear from you!

To get posted on ABDO & Daughters website E-mail us at "mystate@abdopub.com"

Index